GO AWAY!

WHAT NOT TO SAY

By Janine Amos and Annabel Spenceley
Consultant Rachael Underwood

Published in the United States by Windmill Books (Alphabet Soup)
Windmill Books
303 Park Avenue South
Suite #1280
New York, NY 10010-3657

Library of Congress Cataloging-in-Publication Data

Amos, Janine
      Go away! : what not to say / by Janine Amos and Annabel Spenceley.
          p.   cm. – (Best behavior)
      Contents: Grandma's story—The store.
      Summary: Two brief stories demonstrate the importance of looking at a situation
from another person's point of view when both of you want the same thing.
      ISBN 978-1-60754-026-7 (lib.)—978-1-60754-044-1 (pbk.)
978-1-60754-045-8 (6 pack)
      1. Social interaction in children –Juvenile literature   2. Problem solving in
children—Juvenile literature   [1. Problem solving 2. Behavior 3. Conduct of life]
I. Spenceley, Annabel II. Title III. Series
      177'.1—dc22

American Library Binding 13-digit ISBN: 978-1-60754-026-7
Paperback 13-digit ISBN: 978-1-60754-044-1
6 pack 13-Digit ISBN: 978-1-60754-045-8

Manufactured in China

Credits:
Editor: Louise John
Designer: D.R. Ink
Photography: Gareth Boden
Production: Jenny Mulvanney

With thanks to our models:
Jill Sharpe, Lucy and Matthew Battersby, Amelia and Louise John, Elizabeth Deller, and
Ellie Carter.

Grandma's Story

Lucy is looking for bugs.

Grandma is reading a story.

Lucy looks up and
wants to join in.
She goes over to
Grandma.

She crawls onto Grandma's lap and pushes Matthew and Amelia away.

"Go away!" shouts Matthew.

How do you think
Lucy feels?

"Matthew, I think Lucy wants to listen, too," says Grandma.

"But she shouldn't push," says Matthew.

Lucy nods. "I'm sorry," she says.

"What could we do?"
asks Grandma.

**What do you think
they could do?**

"Amelia and I can move over and Lucy can sit in between us," says Matthew.

"Yes!" says Lucy.

"Now everyone can see the book!" laughs Grandma.

The Store

Elizabeth is playing store. She puts all the food on the table.

Here comes Ellie. "I'll be the shopkeeper," she says. "You can buy my things."

"Look," says Ellie.
"We can use this money."

"Go away!"
shouts Elizabeth.

Mom comes over.
"Elizabeth you sound
upset," she says.
"What's the matter?"

"Ellie wants to be the shopkeeper – and I'm the shopkeeper!" says Elizabeth.

"But I want to sell things too!" says Ellie.
"Hmm," says Mom.
"So you both want to be shopkeepers?"

"Yes," agrees Elizabeth. Ellie nods.

What do you think they could do?

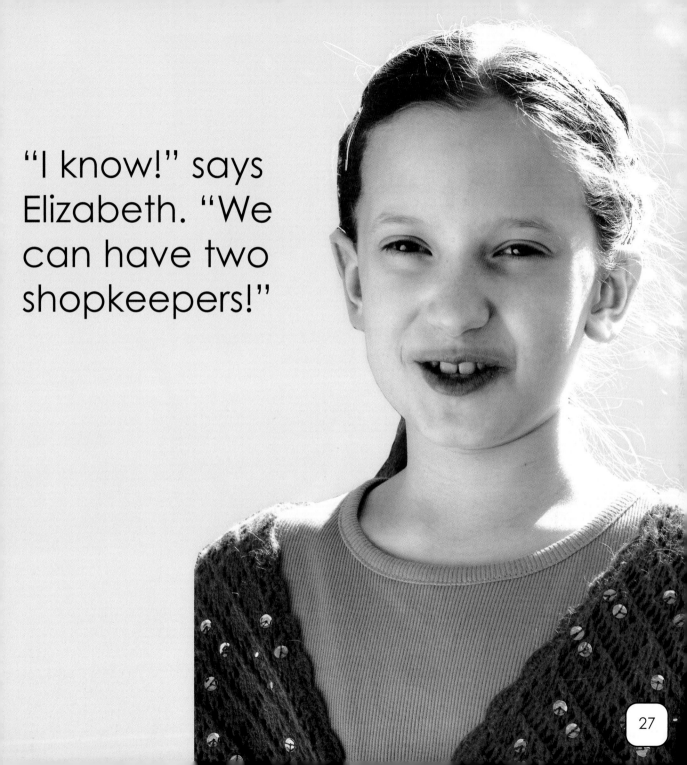

"I know!" says Elizabeth. "We can have two shopkeepers!"

27

"But who will be the customer?" wonders Ellie

Elizabeth looks at Ellie.
Ellie looks at Elizabeth.

They both look
at Mom.

"Mom can!" they shout together.

FOR FURTHER READING

INFORMATION BOOKS

Carlson, Nancy. *How to Lose all Your Friends*. New York: Puffin, 1997.

Krasny Brown, Laurie. *How to Be a Friend: a Guide to Making Friends and Keeping Them*. Boston: Little, Brown Young Readers, 2001.

FICTION

Grindley, Sally. *The Big What Are Friends For? Storybook*. New York: Kingfisher, 2002.

AUTHOR BIO
Janine has worked in publishing as an editor and author, as a lecturer in education. Her interests are in personal growth and raising self-esteem and she works with educators, child psychologists and specialists in mediation. She has written more than fifty books for children. Many of her titles deal with first time experiences and emotional health issues such as Bullying, Death, and Divorce.

You can find more great fiction and nonfiction from Windmill Books at windmillbks.com